Faith

D1644527

St Paul

Faith

THE ETERNAL OPTION

->><-

P

PROFILE BOOKS

First published in Great Britain in 2001 by
Profile Books Ltd
58A Hatton Garden
London ECIN 8LX
www.profilebooks.co.uk

Introduction and text selection copyright
© Jeremy Scott 2001

The selected extracts reproduced in this volume are taken from
the King James (1611), Revised (1881) and modern
editions of the New Testament.

A CIP catalogue record for this book is available from the
British Library.

ISBN 1 86197 372 1

Cover design by the Senate
Cover and frontispece illustration by Clifford Harper
Text design by Geoff Green
Typeset in Van Dijck by MacGuru
info@macguru.org.uk

Printed and bound in Great Britain by
Bookmarque Ltd, Croydon, Surrey

Contents

Introduction   7

Paul explains himself   20

Christ's revolutionary manifesto   24

Christ's pledge . . .   34

. . . Of eternal life   36

Paul accounts for his mission   40

Love – the essence of Paul's message   44

Paul's teaching   46

The Spirit not only conveys power,
    but produces a yield   60

The pledge   62

The inheritance   68

Love: Paul reaffirms the guiding principle
    to his own and Christ's teaching   70

The end of the world   72

Christ's Word   78

The Way   82

Paul's concluding hope   94

Born in AD 10 in Tarsus, a cosmopolitan university city in what is now Turkey, Paul was the son of a devout and highly respectable Jewish family who had improved themselves by acquiring the status of Roman citizens. He was a bow-legged, small, unattractive boy, and after a mediocre education he was sent to study to become a rabbi in Jerusalem, where his rigidly orthodox upbringing led him to join the Pharisees, a Jewish sect whose austere lifestyle was governed by strict adherence to the Law of Moses.

Jerusalem and the surrounding country of Judaea was occupied by a Roman army and run by a Roman governor. The self-serving Jewish authorities collaborated willingly with the civil and military power to maintain the status quo. Theirs was a privileged position in Judaea; by nature they were highly conservative, traditionalist and authoritarian – and so was Paul.

During his studies and after graduation Paul supported himself as a tent-maker, the manual trade he had learned from his father. Once he had qualified, he practised as a rabbi in Jerusalem. Paul was a compulsively hard worker, uncompromising and zealous, and was noticed approvingly by the authorities from early on. In their eyes, this sanctimonious young prig looked as if he might be useful at a time when they were faced by the problem of a revolutionary cult.

This cult, whose members were called Christians, appealed to deprived and disaffected elements of the population and had grown to pose a serious challenge to the establishment. When their leader, Christ, was executed, it was thought that the seditious sect which had grown up around him had finally been wiped out, but, disturbingly, this was not the case. Following rumours that Christ had been seen alive again on earth, the number of Christians increased alarmingly.

Government efforts to eradicate the movement were stepped up. Ruthless measures were instituted, houses were raided, many people taken into custody and whipped; exemplary punishments were handed out. Among those arrested was a man named Stephen, who was brought before the court on a charge of blasphemy. His attitude was not one of contrition;

instead 'with his face lit up', he made a defiant speech, provoking his judges and the crowd to fury. Incensed, the mob seized him and rushed him out to stone him.

It is at this moment that Paul, aged in his late twenties, steps on to the pages of history for the first time. In that confused, hysterical scene reeking of sweat and blood, at whose centre a man is being pulped to death, Paul stands apart – a voyeur. He is guarding the stoners' coats and watching the violence in a thrill of excitement, pleasure and satisfaction.

In Paul, the religious authorities had found the ideal employee for their operation to exterminate the Christian sect. He was an excellent organiser, indefatigable, highly motivated and a workaholic. Sober, dependable, single-minded and rigidly orthodox, he was the perfect bureaucrat. Functionaries of this sort have always been useful during pogroms; it was just such men who made the trains run on time to Auschwitz.

The ruthless punishment exacted on members of the cult and Stephen's public execution largely succeeded in driving the Christians out of Jerusalem. Those who remained hidden in the city Paul pursued, arrested and had whipped. When Jerusalem was effectively cleansed, he requested permission to extend the operation to Damascus. He obtained official orders to arrest the Christians in that city and bring them bound to Jerusalem for trial.

Damascus was two hundred miles away. Accompanied by an escort of militia, Paul set out on a journey that would take twelve days. His route took him past the Sea of Galilee, the region where the cult of Christianity had originated. As Paul's men followed the road along the shore, they passed through the villages where Christ had recruited his first followers only a few years before.

Leaving Galilee behind them they headed north, climbing into the foothills of the Lebanon mountains. Paul rode surrounded by his soldiers, his orders and letters of authority in his saddlebag and his mind busy with plans for the forthcoming operation. And then . . .

And then something happened. As Paul tells it, suddenly, without any warning, the world split open with light. The light struck Paul, knocked him from his horse and threw him to the ground. Sprawled there in the dust, stunned, Paul – and his companions – heard a voice. The voice demanded, 'Why are you doing this to me?'

Terrified, Paul somehow managed to ask, 'Who are you?' And the voice said, 'I am Christ, and you're hunting me down and trying to destroy me.' The voice ordered him to get up and go into the city, where he'd be told what to do. 'And the men who journeyed with him stood speechless, for though they heard the voice they could see no one. And Paul arose from the earth, and when his eyes were open he could see nothing. So they led him by the hand and brought him into Damascus . . .'

Paul's personality was shattered. He had been broken into fragments, then thrown together again in the space of seconds, but he wasn't in any way the same man. His whole nature, his entire being was changed. He was transformed by what had been revealed to him as, blind and traumatised, he was led by the hand into Damascus.

There, after three days of being unable to

eat or drink, his sight returned to him. Asking to be baptised a Christian, he ate some food, went directly to the city's main synagogue and addressed the crowd, relating what had happened to him and claiming that the executed criminal Christ was the son of God.

It was a recklessly unwise thing to do and understandably it created a commotion. People were well aware of Paul's reputation and the reason he'd been sent here. Now this! It was public drama of the most sensational kind. The Jews were outraged; the official responsible for cleansing the city of Christians had joined them instead. When the authorities in Jerusalem heard what had happened, they issued orders to arrest Paul and bring him back bound to the capital.

Meanwhile, Paul continued speaking in the synagogues, telling the avid crowd of his experience and the extraordinary news about the executed Christ. He spoke with an authority and power which won over many of his listeners, confusing the Jews and fuelling their anger. They worked out a plot to dispose of him. 'They watched the gates day and night to kill him, but their laying in wait was known to Paul. When it was dark, some Christians took him and let him down from the top of the wall, lowering him in a basket . . .' Under cover of night, Paul crept away from the walls of Damascus, hunted and alone, to spend the rest of his life advertising to the world the faith that had been revealed to him.

Paul's betrayal of his employers excited extremes of antagonism and hostility. For him to become a member of the Christian sect and start preaching its message infuriated everyone of power and influence. His actions threatened the Roman government by proclaiming a greater emperor than Caesar; they threatened the Jews in their orthodox religion; and they threatened the rich and successful by seeming to say that, in this new scheme of things, they counted for less than publicans, harlots and even children. Paul was pursued relentlessly, arrested and subjected to continuing violence. The Jews never forgave him.

He travelled continually. His journeys took him through the lands we now know as Israel, Syria, Turkey, Macedonia and Greece, and finally, at the end of his odyssey, to Rome. He was, in the truest sense of the word, a man with a mission. In towns containing Jewish communities he found hearers who could relate to what he was saying. There was a Jewish tradition about the coming of the Messiah. But in other, remoter places with non-Jewish inhabitants, the reaction to this dusty figure limping out of nowhere with his extraordinary story was blank incomprehension and amazement, followed invariably by hostility.

Sometimes he rode a donkey, but more often he went on foot. He was without money. When he reached whatever town was his destination he would stay there, working as a maker of tents and sails to support himself while he did as he had been instructed and publicised the faith.

Everywhere he met with difficulty, opposition and worse. In Athens he was laughed at, in Iconium stoned and in Philippi whipped, clamped into stocks and locked up. His travels and his hardships continued for thirty years, but his courage and diligence never faltered. His whole nature had been transformed, but he was still the perfect civil servant.

At last Paul returned to Jerusalem. Within a week of his reappearance in the city he was arrested. It was festival time and Jerusalem was packed. His arrest caused a riot from which he was rescued by the Roman duty officer calling out the guard – who promptly re-arrested him.

He was tried before a Jewish court for bringing non-Jews into the Temple's inner court – an offence which carried the death penalty. The evidence was false and provoked another riot, from which he was again rescued by Roman troops. For his own safety he was transferred overnight to Caesarea, sixty miles away; there he was arraigned before the Roman governor. The Jerusalem Jews with their lawyers argued for a change of venue; the governor, anxious to placate them and end this troublesome affair, formally asked Paul if he was prepared to be tried in Jerusalem.

'I have done no wrong to the Jews, as you very well know,' Paul answered defiantly. 'And if I am innocent not you, not any man, can hand me over to them.' And then he played his last card: 'I appeal to Caesar.' As a Roman citizen, this was his right, but the governor was new in office and he was disconcerted by this case's possible repercussions. He consulted with his lawyers while Paul's accusers waited expectantly. Just when they thought they finally had Paul, they were foiled. 'Have you appealed unto Caesar?' said the governor: 'Then unto Caesar you shall go.'

He was sent under guard to Rome. In all his travelling, he had been nowhere that resembled this. Rome was a city like no other – the imperial capital, the centre of an empire stretching from Turkey to the British Isles, a teeming international metropolis of splendour and slums where the traffic was so acute that the use of wheeled transport was prohibited during daylight hours, and so noisy throughout the night it was almost impossible to sleep.

For two years Paul remained in Rome under house arrest, waiting for his case to come before the Emperor Nero, who had a record of instability and had already shown himself no friend of Christians. Paul's courage was as high as ever, but he was an old man now, stooped and worn from years of hard travelling. His eyesight was failing and he was tired.

While awaiting trial, he wrote letters to the various communities he had founded around the eastern Mediterranean which were now active 'churches'. In one letter he asks for some books and a cloak he left in Troas. He's cold, and his witnesses have deserted him. 'Only Luke is with me now,' he says sadly. He doesn't know what awaits him, but he fears the worst.

His final letter is his last testament. He is single-minded to the end, intent only on fulfilling the mission he was charged with so many years before: 'You know my teaching, and you know my purpose, my faith, my steadfastness; you know all that befell me at Antioch, Iconium, Lystra, and the persecutions and sufferings I went through, from which the Lord rescued me. And you know my enduring love and care for you. Now you must keep to what I have taught you, hold on to what you know to be true. Hold on to the Word and the sacred writings which give wisdom through faith in Christ.

'And in the presence of God and Christ Jesus I urge you to pass on the Word. Never give up your faith and its teaching, for a time will come when people seek only novelty and false prophets, when they abandon truth and turn to myths. So, above all, be courageous and faithful in your work . . .' Paul reaches the end and adds his parting lines: 'As for me my life is already drawing to its close and the time of my departure is at hand. I have fought a good fight, I have finished my course, I have kept the faith . . .'

And here, as Paul completes and signs his last letter on the eve of his trial, the curtain falls across our view of him. We do not know his end; we know only the effect of his life and his teaching, which transformed the revolutionary faith of an obscure Jewish sect into a world religion practised to this day.

Paul's teaching and his constant point of reference is the message of Christ. Where this message is expressed by Christ in his own words, rather than interpreted by Paul, this is indicated in the following pages.

*P*aul explains himself

-+>-<+-

What I'm going to say now is not prompted by the Lord but said by me in a sort of madness. I've listened to so many others boasting of their achievements that I shall myself; I can be as brazen as they are.

Are they servants of Christ? So am I. And more so, for I have worked harder than any, I have been imprisoned more often and whipped more frequently, often almost to death. On five occasions I received the thirty-nine lashes from the Jews, three times I was beaten with sticks, once I was stoned. I've been shipwrecked three times, once I was twenty-four hours in the open sea. Travelling constantly, I have been in danger from rivers and floods, from bandits, from my own countrymen and from pagans. I've known exhaustion, pain, long vigils, thirst, going without food, cold and lack of clothing.

God knows I am not lying to you about any of this.

The word revealed

What you have to understand is that this Word I am passing on to you is not a human message told me by men, but something I learned only through revelation.

You know of **my career** as a practising Jew, how merciless I was in persecuting the Church of God, how enthusiastic I was, and how much harm I did it. Then God chose to reveal his son to me so that I might spread the Word about him to those who did not know . . .

Language of irrationality

My orders are to explain the Word, but not in the terms of philosophy, by which it cannot be expressed. The language of the cross is without either sense or meaning to those who are not already on the way . . . but those who are see it as the path leading to salvation.

If it was God's wisdom that human wisdom should not know God, it was because God wanted to save those who have faith in the absurdity and sheer illogicality of the message that we preach.

Christ's revolutionary manifesto

→>-<←

The basis of everything that Paul taught lies in the revolutionary manifesto issued by Christ some thirty years before Paul's experience outside Damascus. This promotes a radical re-ordering of human values, a complete inversion of established rules and attitudes. Here are the main propositions of that manifesto as proclaimed in Christ's own words . . .

The spirit of the Lord is upon me for he has appointed me to bring the Word to the poor, to heal the broken-hearted, to show freedom to captives, give sight to the blind, healing to the hurt and damaged.

And to preach the acceptable year of the Lord.

Declaration of intent

Do you suppose I have come to bring peace to the world? No, it is not peace I have come to bring but division.

For I have come to set a man against his father, a daughter against her mother, a daughter-in-law against her mother-in-law. A family shall be divided, and a man's enemies will be those of his own household.

I am come not to bring peace on earth, but a sword.

Christ's words

The power of God

He that is mighty has done great things
He has scattered the proud
in the vanity of their hearts.
He has put down the mighty from
their seats,
and exalted them of low degree.
He has filled the hungry with good things,
and the rich he has sent empty away.

Christ's words

The new order

Happy are the poor,
for yours is the Kingdom of heaven.
Happy are you who are hungry,
for you shall be filled.
Happy are you who weep now,
for you shall laugh.
But beware you who are rich,
for you have received your consolation.
Beware you who are full,
for you shall hunger.
Beware you who laugh now,
for you shall weep.

Christ's words

New values

Blessed are the meek,
for they shall inherit the earth.
Blessed are those who hunger and thirst
for what is right,
for they shall be satisfied.
Blessed are the merciful,
for they shall have mercy shown them.
Blessed are the pure in heart,
for they shall see God.
Blessed are the peacemakers,
for they shall be called the children
of God.

Christ's words

Vengeance

You have heard it said of vengeance, 'An eye for an eye, and a tooth for a tooth,' but I am giving you another rule: Offer the wicked no resistance, but if someone strikes you on the right cheek, offer them the left as well. If they take away your coat, give them your cloak also.

Whoever asks you to go a mile with them, go with them two. Give freely to any who ask, and from those who would borrow do not turn away.

Christ's words

Forgiveness

Bless them that curse you, do good to those that hate you, forgive your enemies.

If you forgive others, your heavenly Father will forgive you. But if you do not forgive others, neither will your Father forgive you.

Christ's words

Insouciance

Pay no heed to your life and body, what to eat or how to clothe yourself. Is not life more than food and the body more than clothing?

Observe the birds; they neither sow nor reap nor store food in barns, yet your heavenly Father feeds them. Are you not worth much more than they?

Christ's words

Carelessness about tomorrow

Why worry how you will dress?

Think of the flowers in the fields, they do not work or spin, yet even Solomon in all his glory was not robed like one of these.

So do not ask, 'What are we to eat? What are we to drink? How are we to be clothed?' Your heavenly Father knows you need these things.

Take no thought for tomorrow, tomorrow will take care of itself. Sufficient unto the day is the evil thereof.

Christ's words

Christ's pledge . . .

✦➤◄✦

Retailed to the world by Paul, as expressed by Christ.

I tell you this . . .
Ask and it will be given to you; search and you will find; knock and the door will be opened to you. For the one who asks always receives, the one who searches always finds, the one who knocks will always have the door opened to them.

. . .*Of eternal life*

—>—<—

I am the bread of life.
She or he that comes to me shall never hunger, and whoever believes in me shall never thirst.

Living water

If anyone is thirsty let them come to me.
Let anyone drink who believes in me, for by doing so they shall become a fountain of living water.

Christ's words

An everlasting source

Whoever drinks water becomes thirsty again. But those who drink the water which I give will never thirst again. It will be to them a spring providing eternal life.

Christ's words

Paul accounts for his mission

→>-<←

Brothers and sisters, I have been commanded to pass on to you the truth, the same truth as was revealed to me on the road to Damascus – namely that the reason Christ died was for *us*.

He was buried, but then returned again to life and was seen on earth, first by one, then a dozen, then by a crowd of more than five hundred people.

Lastly he appeared to me as well. To me! It is as if I have been born again against all odds, for I am the least of the apostles. Indeed I am not worthy even to be called an apostle because I persecuted the church of God. But by the grace of God an apostle is what I am, and the grace he gave me has not proved fruitless.

New contract

The key to Paul's teaching was the new contract between God and earth's people. This contract, which was brought to the world by God's son and messenger Christ, superseded the Jewish laws on which Paul had been raised, and which until that moment he had followed scrupulously. It was addressed not just to Jews, but to 'pagans' or non-Jews also. The offer was open to all people, to the whole world.

The new contract stated that to qualify for life after death it is necessary to accept that Christ was indeed the son of God, and to live our life by two instructions:

1 To behave toward others in the same thoughtful and kindly fashion as, in an ideal world, we would like them to behave toward us.
2 To honour and love God above all things.

*L*ove – *the essence of Paul's message*

→>·<←

I will show you a more excellent way . . .
But though I speak with the voice of men and of angels and do so without love, I am no more than sounding brass or a tinkling cymbal. If I have the gift of prophecy and understand all mysteries and all knowledge, and though I have faith enough to move mountains but am without love, I am nothing. And though I give away all I own to feed the poor, and even give my body to be burned, without love it serves for nothing.

Love is patient and is kind, love does not boast and does not take offence, rejoices not in evil but rejoices in the truth; bears all things, believes all things, hopes all things, endures all things. Love never fails.

Paul's teaching

-»-><-«-

For thirty years Paul travelled continually to fulfil the mission he had been charged with: to promote the faith.

In each place where he stopped, his method was usually the same. He found the cheapest lodging and looked for work. On Saturday he would turn up at the synagogue and start to talk. He always found hearers and invariably what he said upset the Jewish elders and resulted in him being thrown out. He was then obliged to speak outdoors, or clandestinely in a private room to the handful of listeners who followed him to form small, shaky communities held together by the faith he had inspired in them.

There are a variety of abilities, but they all come from the same spirit which works in different ways in different people.

One may possess the gift of wisdom, another particular knowledge, another the gift of teaching; in another perceptiveness, in another communication and understanding.

All these come from the same source, from the one Spirit distributing them as he chooses.

No one is an island

Our abilities differ, each has a different usefulness.

In the same way our bodies are made up of different parts, each of which has a separate function; but in our unity in Christ these come together to form one body. And, as parts of it, we belong to one another.

Use of your ability

Employ your abilities for the purpose for which they have been given you. If you have a gift to manage others, manage diligently; if your gift is teaching, teach with discrimination.

But do not delude yourself about your own importance or become self-satisfied. Judge yourself soberly and objectively against the standards God has set us.

Openness to others

Be attentive and kind to each other, let your love be without pretence. Not slothful in business, fervent in spirit, and serving the Lord; joyful in hope, patient in adversity, instant in prayer.

Be open to others. Rejoice with them that rejoice, weep with those that weep, be gentle to those of low estate.

Love of money

We brought nothing into this world, and it is certain we can carry nothing out. If you have food and clothing, be content. Those who long to be rich become caught up in foolish and destructive ambitions, and pierce themselves with many disappointments and sorrows.

For not money but the *love* of money is the root of all evil.

Wealth and possessions

Money itself is neither good nor evil: either out-come depends on how the individual uses it. But love of money and the relentless pursuit of material possessions warp the individual's judgement and divert her or him from the path of faith. This is what Christ has to say on the subject . . .

Possessions

Lay not up for yourselves treasures upon earth where moths and rust destroy them and where thieves can break in and steal.

But store up treasures for yourself in heaven where neither moths nor rust destroy, and where thieves cannot break in and steal.

Success and wealth

Let those who are rich and successful beware they do not despise those who are neither. Warn them not to put their trust in money and possessions, which are uncertain and unreliable, but in the living God who alone will provide us with all we need.

Counsel them to do good and share their wealth, that they may lay down a solid foundation against the time to come, and inherit the true life which endures forever.

Christ's words

We reap how we sow

If we sow meanly in our lives, the harvest
we gather also will be mean; if we sow gen-
erously our harvest will be plentiful.

So let everyone act toward others how
they will, but not grudgingly or through
obligation. God loves a cheerful giver.

He who provides seed for the sower and
bread for food will provide as much seed as
you require. There is no need for prudence
in how you sow; God's generosity is unlim-
ited. He will provide all you need and to
spare, so you may in turn be generous to
others and your good actions yield you
their full harvest.

Christ's words

Justification by faith

Without faith, says Paul, good deeds count for nothing. It is faith alone that provides the passport to eternal life.

Before faith we were subject to the rule of law and ignorant of the faith that would be revealed to us in time. The law was our guardian, guiding us towards that moment when we might be justified by faith.

Now that time has come. We have no further need of a guardian but are free, for all of us are become children of God through faith in Christ.

Justification . . .

Let me explain it like this: an heir, while she or he is still a minor, is no different from a slave. For they remain under the rule of tutors or a guardian until they reach that age, set by their father, when they will inherit.

In the same way we, before we came of age, were slaves to the elements which compose this world. But at the appointed moment God sent his son, born of a woman, to redeem those living under the law so we could be adopted as God's children.

. . . is salvation

Therefore, being justified by faith we have peace in God through our Lord Jesus Christ. By whom we have access to faith, so can look forward to God's glory.

Meanwhile we can derive some glory from our own trials, for enduring tribulations leads to patience, and patience brings perseverance, and perseverance hope. And that hope is not false, for it is the love of God kindled in our hearts by the Holy Spirit which has been sent to us.

The Spirit

This is the agent of God, a force which can lodge within the individual to both inspire and defend him or her in the world. Here it is promised by Christ to all who choose to have faith in him . . .

I shall ask the Father and he will give you another advocate to be with you forever, the Spirit of truth whom the world cannot receive since it neither sees nor knows him. But you know him, for he is with you and in you.

*The Spirit not only conveys
power but produces a yield*

✦

The fruits of the Spirit are joy, peace, patience, kindness, goodness, trust.

So, since the Spirit is our life, let us be directed by the Spirit in all things.

*T*he pledge

→>-<←

Paul promises that death is not the end.

We know that when this tent of bones and flesh we inhabit here is folded up, there is a house awaiting us which is not made by human hands but built by God.

It is in the assurance that our mortality will be taken up into eternal life that God has given us the pledge of the Spirit.

The kingdom of God

Central to the faith Paul publicises is the idea of the kingdom of God. To attain that kingdom is the purpose of life, our true destination.

But nowhere is that kingdom defined, either by Paul or Christ himself. At times it appears to be the place of the afterlife, our home after death. At others, a perfected earth where poverty and suffering no longer exist, and whose inhabitants have come to live in peace and harmony with each other. And then at other times it seems not a place but a state of inner being, a wholeness and generosity of spirit that is not so much a passport to the kingdom as the kingdom itself.

Precisely what that kingdom is remains undescribed. The way to it, however, is clearly indicated. The same road as the path to enlightenment laid down by Buddhism, it leads inward. 'Learn to despise outward things and give yourself to things inward and you shall perceive the kingdom to come in you.'

Here is what Christ says about it . . .

The kingdom is like a treasure hidden in a field which, when a man finds, he hides again and goes off in great joy to sell all he has so he may acquire that field.

Again, it can be compared to a merchant searching for precious pearls who, when he finds one of great value, sells all he owns to buy it.

What else can I compare it to? It is like a grain of mustard, the smallest of all seeds. Yet once it is sown it grows in time into a great tree where the birds of the air come to find shelter in the shade of its branches.

The way to the kingdom

Seek to enter to the kingdom by the narrow gate for the other road which many follow is a broad and easy highway leading to death and nothingness, whereas the way to life is through a narrow gate on to a difficult path, and there are few who find it.

Christ's words

When will it come?

The appearance of the kingdom is not to be observed with the eyes. Watch as you may, you will not see it come. No one will be able to say, 'Look, it is here, or over there!'

Why is this so? It is because the kingdom of God is *within* you.

Christ's words

The inheritance

-->-<--

To have faith is to become a child of God, and an heir.

All who are moved by the Spirit are no longer slaves but have come to be the children of God. And if we are his children we are his heirs also; heirs of God and co-heirs with Christ, sharing his sufferings so as to share his glory.

The sufferings we endure in our worldly life are as nothing compared to the glory that is going to be revealed to us. I tell you that the whole of creation is trembling with expectation, eagerly awaiting the moment when God's children will be revealed.

*L*ove: *Paul reaffirms the guiding principle to his own and Christ's teaching*

+>+<+

Love is the key to everything.

Love never fails and never ends. But where there is the gift of prophecy it shall fail, where there is the gift of communication it shall cease, where there is knowledge it shall vanish away.

For now we know only in part, and can foresee only in part, but when that which is perfect is come then that which is partial will be no more. For now we see through a glass darkly, but then we shall see face to face. Now we know in part, but then we shall know fully as we are known.

Only three things endure: faith, hope, and love. And the greatest of these is love.

The end of the world

✦✦✦

When this will occur is unknown, says Paul, but it will be possible to predict for it will be preceded by certain omens.

Earlier, Christ had foretold these . . .

The sun will be darkened, the moon will lose its brightness and stars will fall from the sky; on earth nations in confusion and distress, and people overcome by fear as they await what menaces the world . . .

Paul's warning

The end cannot happen until the degeneration has taken place and the Evil One has appeared, who claims to be made greater than God and worshipped. He will install himself in God's place and claim to *be* God.

I have warned you of this, and you know what holds it back. Evil is at work already, but he who holds it back will be removed before the Evil One appears openly. But when he does, wickedness will be loosed in the world and there will be all kinds of deceptive miracles and wonders misleading those who would not grasp the truth which could have saved them.

The abomination

When you see the abomination of desolation, spoken of by Daniel the prophet, come to occupy the Holy Place (let who reads this understand), that is the moment to escape.

If you are at the top of the house, do not pause to collect your possessions; if you are outdoors do not return home even to pick up your clothes.

Alas for those with babies or children! Pray it will not come in winter, for there will be distress and suffering on a scale the world has never seen before.

Christ's words

Pervasive evil

Take care, let no one deceive you. For at that time many will present themselves claiming to be the saviour.

You will hear of wars and rumours of wars; but stay calm, the end is not yet.

Evil will be everywhere, in many love will grow cold. People will betray one another and hate one another. But she or he that endures to the end will be saved.

Christ's words

How to react in the event

Nation will rise against nation and kingdom against kingdom. There will be earthquakes and famine and plague . . .

But when these things come to pass, stand erect and hold your heads high, for your liberation is close at hand. Watch, and stay alert, praying for strength that you may hold steadfast and endure to come with confidence before God.

Christ's words

Christst's Word

❯❯❮❮

Throughout his years of travelling, wherever Paul stopped to teach, he started a community and founded a 'church' – though the early Christians had no buildings. Instead they would meet in a private house or wherever else they could. In Ephesus, Paul rented a schoolroom after classes ended at 11 a.m. until they resumed at 6 p.m. He taught in the heat of the day to working men and women who had chosen to listen at a time when all reasonable people were taking a siesta.

'Paul dwelt there, teaching the word of God among them.' It was the same word, the same message he'd always transmitted: the story of Christ's visit to earth and the healing and teaching that occupied his short life here. It was the origin and keystone to the faith, not the word but the Word as described in the gospels.

In the beginning was the Word,
and the Word was with God
and the Word was God.
The Word was the true light
That enlightens all.

A man came, sent by God . . .
The Word was made flesh
and dwelt among us.

He was in the world,
and the world was made by him,
and the world knew him not:
But to all who did accept him
he gave power to become Children of God.

Parable . . .

Paul and Christ addressed their teaching to un-educated and illiterate people, and much of it was in the form of illustrative metaphor or parable.

This is Christ's parable about the Word.

Picture a farmer going out to sow his land. As he walks along, scattering seed, some seeds fall by the edge of the path and the birds fly in to eat them up. Others fall in stony places with little soil. These spring up quickly, but when the sun is high they are scorched and wither for they have no roots. Others fall among thorns, and the thorns grow up and choke them.

But others fall on good soil, and grow to yield a fine harvest.

Whoever has ears to hear, let them hear.

The parable decoded

Called on to explain the parable of the sower, Christ did so in the following way . . .

When anyone hears the Word but does not understand it, then comes the evil one and carries off what was sown in his heart. This is the man who received seed by the edge of the path.

The one who received it in stony places is he who hears the Word and receives it with joy. But some trouble or persecution comes and he lets go the faith. The one who received seed among the thorns is he that hears the Word, but the cares of this world and desire for wealth entangle him and overwhelm his faith so he is unfruitful.

But the one who received seed on good soil is that person who hears the Word and understands it. That man or woman will bear good fruit and bring forth a generous harvest for themselves and many others.

The Way

→>-<←

The aim of Paul's teaching was to open his listeners' hearts to the truth revealed by Christ, and persuade them to commit to a new path in life: the Way.

The Way is not easy, but arduous and hard. And to start upon it requires a considerable sacrifice: to renounce our own will and embrace instead the will of God.

Christ explains what the Way involves, and where it leads . . .

If anyone wishes to be my follower, then let him deny himself, take up his cross each day and follow me.

For whoever desires to save his life will lose it, but whoever loses his life for my sake shall save it. What profit is there for a man to gain the whole world and lose his own soul? For whoever is ashamed of me and of my words, then the son of God shall be ashamed of him in the time that will come.

The Way, the Truth, the Life

I am the Way, the Truth, the Life. No one can come to the Father except through me.

If anyone loves me they will keep my Word, and my Father will love them and we shall come to them and make our home with them.

Christ's words

The light on the Way

I am the light of the world.
Anyone who follows me shall not walk
in darkness
but in the light of life.
If you observe my Word
you shall know the truth
and the truth will set you free.

Christ's words

Humility: the role of one who walks the Way

You know that, among the pagans, it is the princes who rule and the great and powerful who exercise authority.

But it shall not be so with you. No, anyone who wishes to be first among you must become your servant; whoever would be chief, let them be your servitor.

For so it is with the son of God. He came not to be served but to serve, and to give his life as a ransom for many.

Christ's words

Status on the Way

The followers of Christ came to him to ask,
'Who has the greatest status in the kingdom
of God?'

Christ called a little child and set him in
their midst saying, 'I tell you solemnly that
unless you change and become again like a
little child you will never enter into the
kingdom. Whoever makes themselves as
little as this child, the same is greatest in
the kingdom of God.'

Christ's words

Productivity upon the Way

I am the true vine, and my Father is the cultivator.

Every branch in me that bears no fruit he cuts away, and every branch that bears fruit he prunes so it may bear yet more. You are pruned already through the Word I have spoken to you.

Live in me, as I live in you. As the branch cannot bear fruit unless it remains part of the vine, neither can you unless you remain in me.

I am the vine, you are the branches. If you live in me and I in you, you will bear much fruit. But, cut off from me, you can do nothing.

Christ's words

The harvest along the Way

Is there not a saying:
Four months and then the harvest?
Look around you at the fields,
They are ripe, ready to harvest now.
And there is another saying:
One sows, and another reaps.
I send you out now to reap
a harvest you have not sown.
Others have sown it
and now you reap their labour.

Christ's words

The Way leading to eternal life, indicated by Paul, is difficult — even dangerous. But the woman or man who walks it will be accompanied by the Spirit, which will guard them and which can in some circumstances invest them with an actual power.

Here is Christ's promise of that power . . .

Truly I say this to you:

She or he that has faith in me shall be able to do the works that I do, and even greater works.

If you ask anything *in my name*, I will do it.

Christ's warning . . .

If the world hates you, remember that it hated me before it hated you.

If you belonged to the world, the world would love and welcome you as one of its own. But because you do not belong to the world, because I have chosen you out of the world, therefore the world will hate you.

But a time will come when you will be persecuted for your faith, a time when anyone who kills you will think they are doing a service for God.

I tell you this so you may be prepared.

. . . and his last word

Believe me when I tell you this:

My words are not my own, they are the words of the One who sent me. It is not I but the Father who lives in me who speaks these words . . .

Paul's concluding hope

✦✦✦

Whatsoever things are true, whatsoever things are honest, whatsoever things are just, whatsoever things are pure, whatsoever things are lovely, whatsoever things are of good report, if there be any virtue, and if there be any praise, I ask you to think on these things.

And if what I have been saying means anything to you, if love has any influence upon you, or the Spirit we have in common can persuade you, then let us share in this same faith and purpose that I disclose to you.

That this should be so would fulfil my joy.

Other titles from the 'Illuminations' series

Power
by Machiavelli
The notorious master of the subject sets
out his timeless rules on how to get it, use it
and hold on to it.
ISBN 1 86197 353 5

Love
by Vatsyayana
The Indian sage and compiler of the world-
renowned *Kama Sutra* presents his
stimulating and enduring guide to erotic
technique.
ISBN 1 86197 358 6

Happiness
by Marcus Aurelius
The Roman philosopher-emperor describes
his Method to achieve happiness, find inner
peace and change your life for the better.
ISBN 1 86197 367 5